Tails from the ARK

Written by:
Roberta Simpson

Illustrations by:
John Butler

Published by Carpenter's Son Publishing, Franklin, Tennessee

Published in association with Larry Carpenter of Christian Book Services, LLC
www.christianbookservices.com

Illustrated by: John Butler

Edited by: David D. Troutman

Cover and Interior Layout Design: Suzanne Lawing

Printed in the United States of America by Worzalla

978-0-9832846-2-8

Preface

After writing *Nana's Bible Stories*, I was trying to think of different animals in the Bible. I asked my grandson Nathan, who was twelve at the time "What animals are in the Bible besides Balam's donkey and the donkey that Jesus rode on?" His reply to me was "Nan! The Ark!" We had a discussion about writing a book about the animals on the ark, and he even gave me the title – Tales From the Ark. He also said later, "You could also call it, Tails from the Ark." I did love the names, and one day, when I began to write the book he surprised me again by saying "Nan, you could teach the Fruit of the Spirit to children through the animals!"

I was totally taken aback, and excited about the idea, and thrilled at the same time. What a wonderful idea!

So here we are with a book called *Tails from the Ark*, teaching children all about the Fruit of the Spirit, through the animals.

It has been fun! So – Thank you Nathan, for your idea, and I am thankful and grateful for your inspiration!

It has been wonderful for me to have had five wonderful children, and nine wonderful grandchildren.

It has been because of them, that I began telling stories to them when they were little, and am now on an adventure of writing Children's Books.

I also thank all of my family including my wonderful husband, who has been such an encourager!

So – to my children, grandchildren and children everywhere, I wish that you all will enjoy these stories, and learn great lessons in life that will be with you always.

Love and blessings from Roberta Simpson - Nana

Table of Contents

Bird's Eye View ~ Faithfulness

Nana: I am sure that one of the first Bible Stories you ever heard was the story of Noah's Ark. Did you ever have questions like "how did the animals line up and go into the Ark?" and "what was it like to see and feel rain for the first time?" I always wondered about those things too. In these stories, we are going to imagine what it might have been like for the animals and people who lived on Noah's Ark and I like to imagine that while they were on the Ark, God used everyday things in their lives to teach them what they needed to know.

We all need special qualities in our lives to make us better people. The Bible calls these qualities Fruit of the Spirit because these ways of acting and thinking grow easier when we let God's Spirit work in our hearts. We will notice that Noah learned what faithfulness to God was all about before one drop of rain had fallen. Faithfulness is the ability to keep your promises and do the right thing, even when it is hard. Not only does Noah learn how to be faithful, but he learns that God is always faithful.

Arnie was the name of the dove that Noah sent out from the Ark, to see if the land was dry after the flood. He and his wife were one of the many birds who lived on the Ark.

Arnie was always interested in the Ark. He had even heard stories from his grandfather about the Ark. He had heard him say, "Noah has been building this Ark since my grandfather's grandfather was a chick, and he has been doing it just because God told him to do it. No one else cares about God but his family, but Noah doesn't let that stop him." My grandfather would continue, "I wish you little chicks would learn some of that faithfulness quality from him!"

Arnie knew that he was not always reliable. Many times he would interrupt his chores by chasing a bug, or stop to nibble on some yummy berries. Mr. Noah had a secret, a secret that would keep him faithful no matter what!

Many times Arnie and his friends would perch in a tree nearby and watch the Noah family hard at work.

Each day, the neighbors would shout and laugh at the Noah family. They would tease his sons without ceasing.

The people of that day were rather wicked. They were violent, rude and selfish. Noah and his family were so different from their neighbors – kind, gentle but firm, and full of love. And they were absolutely faithful to the God they all loved.

Even Mrs. Noah was laughed at. One day Mrs. Noah was approaching the well to get water, when she overheard the women talking and laughing about her. Poor Mrs. Noah, she burst into tears, and ran back down the hill without her water.

Sometimes children, our faithfulness is tested. There are times when we know He is calling us to be faithful to Him, when others are trying to get us to do something that we know is wrong. In these times, God wants us to be faithful. Even when you are being teased and made fun of, just remember God is faithful and He loves you so much!

As time went by, the Ark got bigger and bigger. The bigger it got, the more the animals and birds talked about the coming rain, and the flood that would follow. They would listen in many times to Noah and his family talking about these things.

Of course, no one knew what rain looked or felt like, and after a while they would just shrug, and start talking about something else.

One day Arnie was in a tree near the Ark. He saw that the Noah family had begun to move all kinds of things into the Ark. First there was furniture, and then loads and loads of food. "Well," said Noah, "The Lord has told me that the flood will come in seven days. We must hurry, and get all the food on board, and then the animals."

Arnie flew home quickly, full of excitement. "Hurry, we need to line up in the nearest tree to the Ark," he said to his wife. "Noah is ready, the Ark is ready, and he is going to be calling all the creatures onto the Ark shortly. Wow, Noah is the picture of faithfulness. He built that Ark no matter what. He has been faithful to God, even though all the people around him have given him a hard time."

It took Noah many years to prepare for the flood that was to come. He never knew what to expect, but he was faithful to God and to what God had called him to do. No matter what, we can be faithful. If we are faithful in the little things, God will trust us with bigger things. Life with God is an adventure. We may never know what's next? The story of Noah and the flood is recorded in Genesis 6:11-8:19.

I can hardly wait to tell you what happened next! All I can tell you is that when Arnie awoke the next morning, he and his wife got the shock of their lives. All they could see from their tree was an Endless Line!

The Endless Line ~ Patience

Can you imagine what it must have been like to see a line of animals as far as the eye could see? Two of every kind of animal? Would you be frightened, or just amazed? The people of Noah's day must have really wondered what was going on. I bet they stayed in their houses that day behind closed doors! Now if you had been in the line with the animals, you would have needed another fruit of the spirit: Patience. Patience is the ability to wait without complaining, angry or upset. You know how hard it is to wait your turn for a toy or game? Sometimes it seems like your turn will never come. It must have been even harder to wait in line with all of those animals as they waited to get into that enormous ship.

Arnie was dreaming of delicious little worms crawling towards his beak, when he awoke with a start at a loud noise. "What in the world...?" He nudged his wife with his beak. "Oh my goodness me, look at that line of animals. I have never seen anything like that in my life!" Arnie's wife, rubbing her sleepy eyes with her wings, was amazed, her beak dropping open. "Oh my! Oh my!" was all that she could say.

Arnie flew from his tree, until he found the front of the line, and there in total charge of everything were Mr. and Mrs. Lion. They were standing very near to the Ark, and all the other animals were in line behind them.

There were large animals and small animals. Arnie had never seen so many colors, shapes and sizes of animals in his whole life. Some animals were very young and of course there were all kinds of birds. The birds didn't wait in line

behind the other animals. They mostly sat on top of the largest animals in little groups. It was an amazing sight!

Then Arnie noticed something else very unusual – there were no other people anywhere besides the Noah family. No one was plowing the fields, or getting water at the well. Even the children weren't playing outside. When Arnie flew over to the nearest house to take a look, he realized that the people were peeping out from the windows. He realized they were terrified of all of the animals.

Many were peeping out from their shut windows, behind curtains. They could not believe what they were seeing. Many of them felt that something strange was happening, and that life would never be the same again!

"I wonder what people are saying?" Arnie thought to himself. He went and perched on a windowsill of a house near the front of the endless line. "What is going on?" he heard someone say. "I don't know!" someone replied. "I have never seen the likes of this! Look at all those animals, as far as the eye can see, and they seem to be lined up in front of the Ark. I always said that Noah was very strange. They must be using some kind of magic."

Arnie shook his head, "That's not magic, it's God!" he twittered. Even after all of these years of Noah telling them about God, they still didn't understand.

Arnie flew back to watch the animals. As he circled, he spotted Mr. and Mrs. Lion in the front of the line. Most of the other animals around them treated the lions with respect. They seemed to be in charge. However, the animals seemed to be a little upset. Arnie decided to fly down and see what was wrong.

"Well!" Mrs. Lion said loudly, so everyone around her could hear. "How long do we have to wait here to get on that Ark? I suppose that is why we are here, right? The sun is too hot, and I am used to that wonderful shady tree we always sit under. And where is the food?" And on and on she went, words pouring out of her mouth like the coming rain.

Mr. Lion just sighed as his wife continued. "I hope we have quarters suited to our status. I'm sure Noah realizes how important we are!"

There were two baby elephants behind the Lions. They seemed to look a bit worried, after listening to Mrs. Lion.

Arnie had had enough. He flew down to the little elephants and landed on one of the ears of the little male, "Hi there! I'm Arnie. I'm sorry you have this place in line so that you have to listen to that snooty Mrs. Lion's complaints.

"I have had just enough of Mrs. Lion's complaints. Her husband is so nice and calm, but she's a real snob. Don't listen to what she says." Arnie fluttered his wings in disgust. "This is going to be a great adventure and it's going to be worth the wait. God loves you and everything is going to be fine!"

"I am going to fly around and hear what the other animals are talking about." By the time he was finished, both little elephants were smiling, and moving their trunks up and down in delight.

"Arnie says that we are on the biggest adventure of all times and that our Creator really loves us and is going to keep us safe!" The male baby elephant shouted to the animals behind him.

Arnie started to laugh. He was laughing so hard that he could hardly fly to his wife. A deliciously funny idea had occurred to him.

"I've thought of a plan that will take Mrs. Lion down a peg or two, and teach her to be a little more humble. Let's convince her that the best place on the ship is the stall between the hippos and the wart hogs."

Arnie's wife started to laugh too, "Oh the mud and the snorting and the smell!" She started laughing so much she almost fell off of her perch.

Arnie stopped laughing as he heard roars and squeaks from further back in the line. There was a big argument going on. Two young giraffes were quarrelling with the animals in front of them, and the ones behind them. In front of them were two monkeys, who I knew to be trouble, and behind them were two young zebras pawing angrily at the grass. They were arguing about what rain would be like.

"I have told you time and time again that this rain that everyone is talking about is green, and it looks like cotton wool!" Mr. Monkey said rudely. His wife looked at him like she would like to smack him with a coconut. "Oh no!" she said. It just might look a little like cotton wool, but it is orange, and when it lands on you, you turn orange!"

Both of the zebras laughed out loud. "You are both wrong. Rain will probably look like leaves and they definitely are going to be purple."

The giraffes shook their heads. "What are you talking about? Why are we arguing? None of us will know what it looks like or feels like until it comes. By that time we will be in the Ark, and will be protected by our Creator." After hearing this from Mr. Giraffe, there was a little silence.

As the day went on and it got hotter, all of the animals were getting more and more impatient. They were quarreling over silly things and grumbling about the wait. Arnie was wondering if some of the animals might end up injuring themselves or each other before the day was finished.

Arnie decided to try to help by flying up and down the line again and encouraging the animals to be patient. Most of them just glared at him, but some of them calmed down and even smiled. Arnie only stopped when he realized that although the line was moving slowly, it was definitely moving and it was time for him and his wife to go take their places. He flew back to his wife and they sat on the baby elephants' backs and watched the lions stalk onto the Ark as if they owned it. Arnie and his wife hid their smiles behind their wings.

So you see, children, we need to have patience. We are always saying to someone "hurry up" or "get on with it," because we are so impatient. Let us just try and be more patient from now on!

I am sure what I have to tell you next will make yourselves think of all the zoos you have been to, and the noise and the smell……well….imagine the reaction when the animals are confined to the Ark.

The animals were trying to imagine what it was like inside the Ark. Well, we will see in the next story how they were so amazed and surprised at what they saw!

The Ark –
Kindness and Gentleness

Have you ever thought of how big the Ark would have had to be to hold all of those animals? It was huge, and it took so long to build. I cannot imagine what it would have been like to have all of those animals on board, and not only that, but to have to feed them as well. Noah and his family had to care for all of the animals on the Ark each day and I am sure that it was a lot of work. We are going to look at Kindness and Gentleness in this story, and we could really say that Noah wins the Gold Prize for his kindness to animals! Are you kind to animals? Remember that God created animals and they are precious to Him too.

After waiting in line the whole day, the animals that had not gotten on board yet began to feel very tired and hungry. You could hear their complaints for miles!

The little monkeys were jumping up and down shrieking loudly. "We have never been so hungry in all of our lives!" one young monkey cried.

A large camel bellowed at the monkey. "You cannot be hungrier than we are!" he answered. "And we are tired too, the sun is going down and it looks like we will be here all night long!"

The animals all perked up when they saw Noah appear on the deck of the Ark. Since they had been at the back of the line, they had not seen him all day.

Noah looked at all of the animals with a smile on his bearded face. "I want to welcome all of you! The Ark is ready, and the rain will begin soon. God has spoken and He wants you all to be safe. He has told me how to build this Ark, so that all of you can fit in comfortably, and be provided for in the best way. When the rains come, we will be safe in here. You have nothing to worry about."

The animals listened quietly. Mr. Noah seemed so very kind and concerned. "So, come on board all of you, and I and my family will show you to your quarters. There is plenty of food and water for all of you, but please do not rush, or shove each other. We have plenty of time!"

Arnie had been quiet all evening. He was feeling very tired, and at this time he was perched in a tree nearby. He could see Noah clearly from his perch, and was all ears as Noah started to speak.

For some time, Mrs. Lion had been complaining, and had started to walk slowly toward the Ark. Of course Mr. Lion and all the other animals had followed. By the time Mr. Noah had come out onto the deck, the animals were very close to the Ark.

When Mr. Noah started to speak, all the animals came to a halt.

After he had welcomed them and described the safety and provisions of the Ark, the animals were silent. Mr. Noah seemed so very kind and concerned. He spoke firmly but lovingly to them all.

Just then, two brown bunnies and two young cats hopped up to the front of the line. Mrs. Lion looked down on these little furry creatures with a frown on her face, and her nose in the air.

"I hope that we can be near each other!" one little bunny said to the cats. "That would be such fun!" a little tabby cat replied with a purr and a meow.

"Get back into the line!" Mrs. Lion said angrily. "You cannot possibly think you small ones can get on board before us!"

Just then one of Mr. Noah's sons came down to where the animals were lined up. He looked down at the two bunnies and the cats, and with one swoop, picked them up in his arms, and went up into the Ark, laughing and nuzzling the little animals with his chin.

Mr. Lion gave his wife a glare, and she did not dare utter even a squeak! She just kept her head as high as she could, and started up the slope to the Ark.

Arnie had been waiting for the right moment to fly onto the Ark. That moment had come, and happily, he and his wife said goodbye to the baby elephants and with a cheerful chirp, flew through the large door.

Boys and girls, the Ark was huge! It was about half as wide as a football field (75 ft) and longer than three football fields put end to end (more than three stories high), and had a deck area the size of 36 lawn tennis courts. Its length was 450 feet, and its width was 75 feet. Its height was 45 feet. It was an amazing building and was made from gopher wood. It was the most perfect vessel to sail on the flood waters. It would be safe in the roughest waters.

Arnie and his wife perched on a beam so they could look down and see what was going on. They were speechless with wonder. The animals were stunned. Their home for the next few months was beautiful! The wood had been sanded smooth, and the decks were filled with roomy stalls with big feeding troughs. Each stall had lots of hay for comfort, and each stall was perfectly designed for the animals that would live there.

Arnie and his wife began to explore this huge kind of a ship. They saw small stalls, tiny stalls, and very large and huge stalls.

"Look at this stall!" said Arnie's wife. "It must be for the giraffes. It is so tall." "Yes!" said Arnie, "And this huge one must be for the little elephants. They grow so quickly, and even though they are young now, they will be large very soon!"

Arnie began chirping in delight. "Look!" he said excitedly. "This must be for us birds." He flew into a room which had lots of pieces of wood put together to look like perches. There was also plenty of food and water, the kind that birds love.

Just then, two young tigers came by, and were shown their cage. "This is very roomy and comfortable." They immediately lay down, yawning. "How kind of the Noah family." Mrs. Tiger sighed. "Yes," said Mr. Tiger. "They have thought of everything. I do not know what this rain thing will be, but I know one thing; we will all be safe."

All of a sudden there was a large roar. You could hear it bellow through the length and breadth of the Ark. The animals all ducked their heads and some of the birds flew off their perches in fright.

"You relax!" Arnie said to his wife. "I bet that that is Mrs. Lion, and I just have to go and see what is happening." He flew off, his wife settling down for the night.

Mrs. Lion was having a temper tantrum and a lion having a tantrum is a very noisy thing! She was pacing up and down in a big comfortable stall, roaring, "I will not, I absolutely will not, be put in a pen next to the Wart

Hogs. We deserve quarters away from everyone. We need our privacy; we need a quiet place to think our thoughts. These little Wart Hogs are far beneath me socially. I repeat, I will not stay in this pen another second."

"My dear!" said Mr. Lion. "Look how comfortable we are. A lovely roomy pen, clean water, and all the food we love to eat. You are so ungrateful! The Noah family have worked so hard to make us happy and safe. They have been so kind to us, and look how gentle and sweet they are to all of the animals. You need to calm down and be grateful!" Mrs. Lion just lashed her tail and continued pacing and roaring.

Not long after Arnie got there, all of the Noah family had arrived at the Lion's pen. The poor little Wart Hogs were cringing in a corner of their pen shaking with fear. Mrs. Lion was so much bigger than them, and her roar made them tremble.

Mr. Noah and his sons went into the Lion's pen, while the wives visited the little Wart Hogs. "You poor little creatures," said Mrs. Noah. "Don't be afraid, we will not let anything happen to you. God brought you here to us, and He loves you and will protect you. You are safe in here." She picked up one of the little hogs, while the other wives comforted the other one.

The Wart Hogs calmed down, while Mrs. Lion was still pacing her pen, glaring at Noah and his sons.

Noah went up to Mrs. Lion. He patted her on her head. "What is wrong with you? You need to calm down. We have thought a lot about where we were to put each animal. I thought you'd be a good influence on the Wart Hogs , since you've always had such lovely manners. It's much too late to move you, and besides we built this pen especially for you lions. None of the other pens would suit you as well. We love all of you, and want to do everything we can to make you happy."

Mrs. Lion calmed down with the sound of Noah's voice and gentle touch. She gave a big sigh, and lay right down. She still would like to have moved away from the Wart Hogs, but she was flattered that Noah had thought she would be a good influence on them. He was right of course. Who knew more about manners than the queen of the beasts?

There are times in our lives, when kindness and gentleness go a long way. In Proverbs 15:1, the Bible tells us that "A gentle answer turns anger away. But mean words stir up anger." When others are mean to us, instead of being mean back, we should show kindness and gentleness, and it can change the other person, and give us peace at the same time.

I wonder what the animals thought when they were in the Ark for a whole week, before the rains came? I believe the Ark would have sounded like a crazy zoo, as the animals would be complaining. Maybe some of the animals felt like abandoning ship!

Where's the Rain? ~ Self Control

Do you know children, that when God shut the door of the Ark, there was no rain for seven days? Can you imagine what was going through the minds of Noah's family and the animals? During that time, Noah must have doubted that he had heard from God, and the animals must have wondered why they were cooped up in the Ark, and not running around in the wild.

Just think about all of the work Noah and his family had to do to keep the animals' stalls clean and to make sure they were all fed! They must have had to get up really early and go to bed as soon as the sun went down. Just keeping your own room clean can be quite a chore can't it? Are you faithful in doing your chores each day?

While waiting for the rain, Noah displayed the Fruit of Self Control. This we need when things are going wrong, and we do not have the answers. However difficult our situation may be, we need to be self-controlled, and put our trust in God.

It was a beautiful morning. The sun was streaming through the windows of the Ark, with the animals waking up one by one. Noah and the family were up very early, checking supplies, and filling up all the animals' troughs.

There was a lot of cleaning up to do also, as you can imagine!

All the animals were in quite good moods that morning, and of course Arnie was flitting around, looking for some adventure.

There was a lot of discussion about the rain. "When is the rain coming?" was the most popular question. "Well, now we are in the Ark, where is this rain?" Mrs. Lion said sarcastically. Everyone ignored her, especially her husband. While Arnie heard a few complaints, and noticed there was some confusion as to what the rain would look and feel like, most of the animals were happy, eating hungrily, and treating each other quite well.

Mr. Noah and his family let the animals out of their stalls in groups, to walk freely on the deck for a few minutes each day, so they could get a little exercise. When the Hippos came out, everyone scrambled out of their way.

With their wide feet and big jiggly bodies, they took up so much room, and looked like they would squash the smaller animals.

It seemed that the day ended so quickly, and before anyone realized, it was night and it was time to eat and go to sleep.

Arnie remarked to his wife. "Well dear, this was a very peaceful day, with nothing to report. I hoped we would see the rain by now. All the animals are rather disappointed." "Oh well", his wife said, "there is always tomorrow." Noah and his family were so tired that night, that they hardly noticed that there was no rain. They lay down on their mats and fell fast asleep.

The next morning was another bright and sunny day....still no rain. The Wart Hogs started to complain. They missed the outdoors and their muddy puddles.

Then the smaller animals complained, and soon the larger animals joined in. This went on for a few days. "Where is the rain?" "Why are we here in this Ark?" "I miss the great outdoors; I don't want to be in here!" On and on it went.

All of a sudden, Arnie noticed Mr. Noah. He looked very cool and calm. Arnie remarked to the little elephants, "He does not seem too worried or concerned that there is no rain, and he is working so hard while we do nothing. Maybe he knows something we don't." The elephants nodded with their trunks.

This particular day was the fourth day, and only Mrs. Noah and her family knew what Mr. Noah was going through.

He had heard the complaints, and noticed that the animals did not look too happy. He saw the way they looked at him, and it scared him a little bit. The one thing he did not need was a rebellion!

Can you imagine children, being on the Ark with all of those animals, lots of them being so big? You would not want them to be angry with you! Mr. Noah must have felt so helpless at times. He knew that when it started to rain, it would rain for 40 days and 40 nights! He probably wondered if he would be able to survive! This is where the Fruit of Self Control came in.

There were a few moments standing on deck in the bright sunshine when he started to doubt whether he had heard from God or not, but when he saw the miracles all around him, such as the dimensions for the Ark, and the way the animals had come in two by two, he knew that he had heard right.

He was determined to continue to trust, and no matter how difficult things appeared, he would be calm and peaceful. With God's help, he would show everyone how to be self-controlled.

It was early in the morning of the sixth day that the real trouble began! Noah was always up early, before anyone else, but today everyone on the Ark was awakened by the loudest noise that they had ever heard!

ROOOOOAAAR!!!!!!!! The noise was terrible, and the Ark vibrated and shook! All the animals trembled, and were afraid.

"It's Mrs. Lion again!" said Arnie. "No one can roar and make a noise like that! Did you notice how the Ark shook?" His wife nodded with her beak, but she was trembling. Arnie covered her with one of his wings while whispering comforting words in her ear.

All of a sudden there was another awful sound. WHAP! WHAP! When Arnie flew to see what this newest noise was, he saw two shaggy white mountain goats butting their heads against the door. "We want OUT!" the lady goat baaed.

"We want to go back outside where there are mountains to climb! There's nothing here to climb but the pile of hay in the hold," complained the male goat and he hit the door with his horned head.

Noah's sons ran quickly to stop anything really bad from happening. "I know it's hard to wait, my friends, but please try to trust God and know that He has a plan and the rain will come in His time," pleaded Noah as he patted their shaggy heads. The door did not seem to be damaged, and in quick time, the goats were escorted back to their pens, with their heads bent down in shame.

Now all of the animals then started to groan and moan. The noise was terrible. Even though they were surrounded with unhappy animals, the Noah family never acted frustrated or upset. As the sun began to set, Noah and the family came to feed and take care of the animals. They were loving, kind, gentle and calm and somehow the animals began to calm down too. They knew in their hearts that some kind of trouble was coming and that they would be well cared for on the Ark. Finally they settled down for the night.

About midnight there was a rumbling in the distance.

Arnie noticed two young panda bears whimpering nearby. He flitted over to them. They had heard the thunder, and they were very afraid. They were clinging to each other, "What is that noise?" said one Panda.

"I don't know, and I do not like the sound and I'm afraid." They both put their soft paws over their ears, lying close to each other. Arnie tried to comfort them, but he also wondered what that strange, frightening noise was.

However, most of the animals were tired, but all were troubled at what they were hearing. Luckily, they were so sleepy, that in no time at all, they heard nothing but the soft, or loud snoring of the animals nearby.

Arnie flew back to his nest and snuggled with his wife. "Is this what rain sounds like?" he wondered. "I'm glad I'm in this strong Ark. Maybe the waiting is over and the adventure is about to begin!" With that thought he dropped off to sleep until much later when the storm really arrived.

The rumbling was getting closer!

Noah could have reacted in anger against the animals, but he did not. Next time you come up against someone or something that causes you anger and pain, remember the Fruit of Self-Control!

Scripture References: Genesis: 6:11-8:19 - God said to Noah, "Make yourself an ark of golden wood....I am going to bring floodwaters on the earth...you and your family are to go into the Ark with two of each animal..."

Galatians: 5:22,23 – But the fruit of the Spirit is love, joy, peace, patience, kindness, goodness, faith, gentleness and self-control.

The Big Storm - Peace

The Fruit of the Spirit we will see in this story is Peace. We feel peace when we relax, and let God take care of us. We need peace when situations are frightening us or making us worry.

Have you ever been in a situation where you feel anger, or you want to say something mean? Maybe someone has said something really mean to you and you want to lash out at them? Well that is when we need peace. Instead of retaliating, or saying something we would be sorry about later, we need to have those fruit of the spirit!

Noah and the animals had never seen rain, or experienced lightening or thunder. Usually when we have a lot of rain, we see lightning and hear thunder and sometimes we are afraid when the thunderstorm seems close to us. Just imagine how petrified the animals must have been.

It was early morning, and dawn had not yet come. The rumblings had been getting closer and louder during the night. Noah and his family were up, speaking together in whispers, wondering if the rumblings meant that the rain was on the way. Every time they heard the rumblings, the animals close to Noah's quarters could hear things shaking near the kitchen. A few times they could hear platters and mugs crashing to the floor, as the Ark would shake. It was frightening!

Just before dawn, Mrs. Noah exclaimed, "Oh, did you see that?" They had been looking through a couple of the windows to the Ark. "I saw a flash of light so bright that it seemed like day!" They had all seen it, and fear crept into them.

Noah had never seen anything like this light that lip up the night sky. He had never heard this terrible rumbling before but he knew he had to be brave and to control himself for the sake of his family and the animals. "No need to be afraid, whatever comes is the plan of God, He will take care of us. This Ark is strong, and God Himself gave me the instructions to build it." Noah put his arm around his trembling wife and began to pray, "Lord, all these things are so new and frightening to us but we know that You are in control and You will take care of us". When the family opened their eyes, they all felt peace flow into their hearts.

In the meantime, the animals were waking up, one by one, listening and watching. Many of them were cowed down in their pens, the fur on their backs rising up. Surely the world was ending! What terrifying stuff rain must be!

Arnie and his wife were cuddled up together on their perch, not liking the sounds they were hearing at all.

All of a sudden there was a crash. The loudest crash that anybody had ever heard, it shook the Ark, and a zig-zag light lit up the sky. People and animals trembled. The next thing they heard was a sound of water running. To the animals, it sounded like a waterfall that they would drink from. To Noah and the family it sounded a bit like taking water from the well and pouring it into a jug.

Noah exclaimed "It's the rain! That is what all of this is about."

The animals that could see out of the windows, tried to describe the rain to the others. "It is water coming down from the sky!" Mr. Tiger said. "Yes, there is so much of it, and it is not green or orange. And you can see through it, just like the water in the stream!"

And it rained, and rained and rained. It did not stop until it had rained for forty days and forty nights.

After a couple of days, they could see the water start to cover everything. They could not see the green grass or the shrubs. Then it started to cover the houses and trees and finally it covered the mountains. After a while they could not see anything at all but water in all directions.

Most frightening of all, as the land disappeared the Ark gave a mighty groan and began to move. As it floated away, it began to sway and rock. It rocked to and fro as it climbed up bigger and bigger waves and Noah prayed that they would not sink! He prayed for confidence so that they wouldn't panic even though everything was so different and scary. He prayed that God would comfort them and bring them peace even when their stomachs felt queasy. As the Ark moved and rocked, some of the people and animals on the Ark began to feel sick. They had never felt anything like this before and their stomachs weren't very happy about it.

Have you ever been seasick? It is not very nice, and sometimes if you are on a boat, it can last for hours! Nowadays they can give you medicine if you feel sick, but in those days, they would not have had such things.

For a couple of days very few of the animals, or even the Noah family, did not feel like eating. There were moans and groans everywhere. There was still a lot of thunder and lightning, but it gradually lessened and died away but the rain continued for more than a month – 40 days and 40 nights! Can you imagine rain like that? I have had rain for two or three days, and that is bad enough! Many times on TV we see floods, and see how bad it can be, water in people's houses, and covering cars.

Noah and his family tried their best to take care and comfort the animals. He gathered his family and spoke to them. "We must try to help the animals. We can comfort them since God has comforted us." Mrs. Noah and their sons' wives would go and pick up the little animals and cuddle them, speaking soothing words to them. Noah and his sons went and patted the larger creatures.

There were two black bears that were cuddled together in their pen, shivering with fright. One of Mr. Noah's sons went in, and spoke kindly to them. "Don't worry, we will not let anything happen to you, we are going to take good care of you!" The bears felt very encouraged. Mama bear said "The Noah family is so peaceful, and I feel peace when I am around them!"

Life went on! Day after day, it rained; they had never seen anything like this ever, but after a while the people and animals got used to it. Then they began to long for the way things used to be – sun, dry land and open spaces. For so long their whole world was just the Ark, the sky and the water raining down.

Weeks had passed when one morning the animals awoke to frantic chirping. "He is lost, I cannot find him! He was right next to me all night, and when I awoke he was gone! Oh dear, where is he?" Arnie's wife was beside herself. Arnie seemed to be lost. His wife had looked everywhere for him. The animals were getting a little annoyed. They did not like to be wakened up like this in the early hours of the morning.

Noah's wife knew just what to do. She came up to Arnie's wife. "I am sure we will find him. He has to be on the Ark, where else would he be?" Arnie's wife sobbing uncontrollably said, "He may have fallen through one of the windows into that water!"

"Stay calm, my dear," comforted Mrs. Noah. "I'll look for him myself." Her calm and peaceful searching soon helped her find Arnie. He was perched in a window looking longingly outside. Over the sound of the rain and the wind, he never even heard his wife and had no idea that he was "lost"!

"I am so glad that I have found you," said Mrs. Noah. "Your wife is looking for you." Arnie looked a bit sad and forlorn. He sighed deeply and said. "Where is the land? Where is the grass and where are the beautiful trees? I am just longing for a nice green perch, and some wriggly worms that I love so much." He sighed again, not realizing that soon enough his longing would be fulfilled!

So children, even in the most difficult times, we can have peace, when we trust in God. We all go though things that we can't control but we can be peaceful when we realize that nothing is out of God's control. He loves us and we can always trust Him to take care of us. Just like Mrs. Noah, we can also use the peace that God gives us to help other people when they are afraid.

God Remembers ~ Joy

Can you imagine being part of the Noah family, and living on that Ark for months and months, and not seeing anything but water? It really shows what Noah's faith was all about. Sometimes we have to go, or are led into the unknown, and it can be a bit frightening. But we see in the Scripture that God remembered Noah. He had not forgotten him or his family or his animals! Let us see what happens next.

After 150 days on the water, everyone was pretty tired of seeing water, water, everywhere! The animals were bored. The Ark was roomy and they all got plenty of exercise and food, but they missed green grass and trees.

Even the most patient of them was getting restless. Now and then, Noah and his family could hear complaining in the form of growls, and sighs, and various animals walking impatiently in their pens. The birds were squawking, and they could hear, from time to time, monkeys screeching.

Things had been the same for so long; it caused quite a stir when suddenly the Ark stopped floating! One day, all of a sudden, there was a grinding noise and a thump. Arnie nearly fell off his perch. The animals started making a commotion while Noah climbed up and looked out to see what had happened. Arnie flew eagerly over and settled on Noah's shoulder.

"What do you see?" asked Mrs. Noah. "We're on top of a mountain! We must be because we're definitely not moving anymore." Noah was right. The Ark had come to rest on the mountains of Ararat.

Surely everything would change now! The animals waited for Noah to open the huge door, but God had not told him it was time to leave.

"What are we waiting for?" sighed a gangly wildebeest. "I can see outside and I can tell you there isn't anything much above this water. There is nowhere to go yet and nothing to eat," said a wise giraffe.

Two and a half months later, as the waters continued to go down, other mountain peaks became visible, but the big door of the Ark remained closed!

It was very unsettling.

Have you ever been in a situation, where it seemed nothing would ever change? Your heart felt heavy, and the circumstances did not seem to get any better? Well, this is what Noah must have felt, and again, he had to have patience, and remember that God had led him this far, and would protect him, and see him through!

Arnie woke up feeling very restless. He had been dreaming again of perching in a wonderful green tree, with lots of lovely leaves and branches, and of course, plenty of wriggly worms to feast on. He awoke, flew to one of the windows and looked out on another dreary day on the water.

Just then, one of Noah's daughters-in-law walked by. Arnie flew over and perched on her outstretched hand. She held Arnie close to her, "Hello little friend. Thank you so much for helping me last night. You found my needle!" Arnie snuggled against her cheek, comforted by her kind words. Noah and his family really cared for all the creatures on the Ark, and somehow they would all get through this.

Suddenly a gust of wind blew her hair around and almost knocked Arnie off her finger. The waves whipped into whitecaps, straw swirled in the pens and the lion's mane was ruffled. God was sending a wind to pass over the earth, to help the water dry up more quickly.

All of a sudden, Mr. Noah started calling for Arnie. When Arnie heard the voice of Noah, he flew to him immediately. He could hear the excitement in his voice, and knew that "something was up!"

Noah opened the window. "Go and see if there is any land anywhere, and then come back to us." Arnie flew out of the window, with the Noah family and many of the animals watching from different windows of the Ark.

There was great excitement! Would Arnie find land? What would he see, and oh, why is he taking so long? People and animals alike were shaking and chattering with excitement.

It seemed like hours had gone by, when all of a sudden, Arnie flew back inside the Ark. Noah was waiting for him, Arnie had nothing to report. Noah drew him back in, and encouraged him with kind words. "Well done Arnie!" said Mr. Noah. "You were so brave to go out all by yourself!" The animals all agreed, and Arnie was a hero to them.

Seven days later, Noah called for Arnie once more and asked him to go for a second look. "You are a strong flier and my daughter-in-law tells me that you have keen eyes! I need you to take another look out there for me. Bring me something to show what is going on outside." Arnie again was thrilled to have such an important job. And once again, animals and humans alike were almost holding their breath, waiting for some good news.

Toward evening Arnie flew back into the Ark, but this time with a fresh olive leaf in his beak.

Well, you should have heard the noise, the lions were roaring, the monkeys chattering, humans were jumping up and down and there was a wonderful time of rejoicing. At last, there were signs of life on the earth again, and hopefully the time of the Ark would soon be over!

There was great joy in the hearts of the Noah family and the animals that night, and it took a long time for everyone to fall asleep.

Isn't it wonderful, when we see the answer to prayer, or something happens to us or one of our friends that brings such joy. What a wonderful fruit of the Spirit Joy is--we cannot do without it!

Land at Last ~ Love

I wonder how the Noah family and the animals felt, knowing that soon they would be leaving the Ark to start all over again on land that was not familiar to them? Would they have been afraid, even just a little bit? Maybe the Ark represented safety to them by this time, and the unknown would have been a little frightening. But you know, God always has a plan, and the earth was once again brand new and exciting!

Another seven days had gone by, and Arnie decided to have a talk with his wife. "I believe Noah may be sending me out again," said Arnie. "And this time I may find dry land, and if so I will not come back." Tears welled up in his wife's eyes. "Don't worry," said Arnie. "If I do not return, it will mean I have found a wonderful place for us. A lovely lush tree, with our favorite worms for us to eat. I will build a nest for us and I will be waiting for you when you come out of the Ark, and then we will start our new life."

Arnie's wife chirped with joy at the idea of her own nest, but all too soon Mr. Noah was calling for Arnie once more. The smell of new grass was in the air as Arnie took off from Noah's finger. Nightfall came, and Arnie did not return.

Everyone knew what Arnie's disappearance meant--there must be trees for a bird to perch in and food for the bird to eat. Surely it couldn't be long now! Arnie's wife felt lonely without him, but she encouraged herself by thinking of green trees, nests and eggs.

In the meantime, wonderful things were happening on the Ark. Mrs. Lion, who had been such a snob when first going on to the Ark, had grown to really love the Wart Hogs! They were so little and many times were very fearful, and sad. She grew to love them, and today, there she was encouraging them, and telling them that they would soon be off the Ark and would have lovely grass to run on, and mud to bathe in! The Warthogs snorted with happiness. They just loved her. She had also been acting like a mother to them.

The animals had really learned the Fruit of the Spirit, and during that time, they had learned to really love and appreciate each other.

The day after Arnie left, Noah opened all the windows and the covering of the Ark. The animals were delighted to see that floodwaters had really receded, and they could see land everywhere. However it was harder than ever to wait another two more long months while the hills grew green and lush. The days seemed to drag by, and the animals could only talk about what they would do when they would be walking on dry land once again.

In the meantime, Arnie had indeed found his "dream tree", and was so excited! He could see the Ark in the distance, and knew it would not be long before they would all be reunited again. He kept himself busy making the best nest he could.

The days seemed long. The animals were all chattering and discussing what they would do when their feet first hit land.

Noah and his family were very excited too. They had been concerned that their food was running out. They discussed what they would do when they got off the Ark, and how they would build their new homes. As excited as the people and the animals were, they were all a little sad at the idea that they would be separated from each other. They had all become such close friends. There was not only joy on the Ark, but love too.

At last, the day came. God told Noah that it was time to leave the Ark. Oh the rejoicing that took place. The Ark once again sounded like a zoo, but for a wonderful reason.

Once the big door was opened, the animals began to walk out onto the beautiful carpet of grass and wildflowers. It took quite a long time, but soon enough all were once more on dry land. There was so much chattering going on. The animals were all overjoyed, and were talking in their animal talk to each other. Many were saying that they would miss each other, and they made plans to meet up later.

Many of the animals and birds went to the Noah family, and nudged them, rubbing their heads on their legs, in thanks for all their loving care. Noah and his family took time to express their appreciation too. They stopped outside the Ark and thanked God for his love, care and protection over the long months.

Suddenly, a beautiful band of colors arched across the sky. It was amazing. No one had ever seen such a thing before. It was God's promise that the world would never again be destroyed by water – the first Rainbow!

Every human's and animal's attention was on the Rainbow, when a commotion in a nearby tree attracted their attention. It was Arnie, chirping away, and looking for his wife. With great joy they were united, animals and humans cheering on each in their own way.

So children, there was great rejoicing that day. And lots of love. God is faithful to His word, and sometimes time goes by and we wonder "why is this taking so long?" Aren't you glad that God always has a plan, just like He did on the Ark? The people and animals were on the Ark for about a year, but God kept them safe and gave them a beautiful new start. Let us all be filled with God's love and peace, and always try and have the Fruit of the Spirit working in our lives."